I Have Eczema

Written & Illustrated By
Jen Greatsinger, RN
Lisa Crosby, LSW, BFA

2015 First edition. Produced by Middle River Studios, LLC, Poplar, WI. Collaboratively written and illustrated by Jen Greatsinger and Lisa Crosby. All rights reserved. No part of this work may be copied or reproduced or transmitted in any form or any means, electronic or mechanical, including photocopy, recording, or by any information storage and retrieval system without written permission of the authors.

To contact the authors write to Middle River Studios, 4259 S. County Road D, Poplar, WI 54864.

ISBN-13:978-1502337931

This book is dedicated to

Maggie

Acknowledgements;
Kara Ronchetti for your editing.
Jason Greatsinger and Amy Seip for your photography.
All of our family and friends for your encouragement and support.

Hi, I'm Emma, and
sometimes I get **really itchy!**

My skin is very dry. Dad says I have eczema.
Mom says it can also be called *Atopic Dermatitis*.

But, Grandma thinks it is **Itchy Monsters**!

All I know is my skin gets...

ITCHY,
and
RASHY,
and
RED!

It drives me wild!

Mom says, "Try not to scratch, Emma."
Dad says, "Please don't pick."

But it is hard to stop! Scratching my prickly, dry skin feels so good.

I scratch, and rub, and...

OH NO,
NOT *AGAIN!*

Dad dabs my sore skin with a wet washcloth.
Ahhh, that feels better. I try to remember that
scratching always makes eczema WORSE.

Today we are going to see the dermatologist. A dermatologist is a doctor who knows a lot about people's skin. It is warm and sunny, so we walk to my appointment.

The dermatologist is friendly and helpful. She carefully checks my skin to see if my eczema is looking better. I am proud when she says, "You have been taking good care of your skin, Emma."

She shows me pictures of things that can trigger my eczema. For example, getting too hot and sweaty makes me itch. "But, everyone is different," she says. She explains that many things can irritate dry skin and what bothers me may not bother someone else!

Next, we look at pictures of a boy with eczema. His skin is very dry and itchy.

When he scratches, his face gets red and rashy.

The dermatologist explains that thick creams and lotions help to keep moisture in our skin.

His dry skin feels better when he puts lotion on it. Just like my skin!

Before we leave, the doctor talks with my parents.
I wonder why she doesn't mention Itchy Monsters?

Maybe,

she doesn't know

about them yet!

On the way home, I see a big fluffy dog. He looks SO soft. I want to pet him! Some people with eczema have allergies. I am allergic to dogs. Grandma reminds me he could be full of **Itchy Monsters.**

Grandma leads me away, but I WANT to pet the dog!
I **stomp** my feet.
I **yell**.
I make **angry faces**.
Uh Oh...

Now I am very itchy. Mom scoops me up in her arms and rocks me back and forth, back and forth. We take deep breaths. When I calm down, my eczema calms down, too. I wave good-bye to the dog!

At home it is time for my skin care. I do skin care every day. Dad puts lotion on me and I put lotion on him, too! Aren't we silly?!

But, I don't always like putting lotion on my skin. Sometimes I cry when the lotion stings me.

I get cranky if the lotion is cold.

And, it is frustrating when my clothes stick to me!

Lotion gets in my hair, too. "Hey lion-hair," Dad smiles. We laugh. He doesn't have enough hair to be a lion! Mom peeks in and tells me it is time for my "wet dressings".

I do wet dressings on days my skin is dry and itchy all over. If just my feet itch, I do "wet socks". Tonight, Mom puts me in warm, wet pajamas, and wraps me in a candy-cane striped towel.

We snuggle on the couch and read stories. My skin feels soft when we finish. Yawn, my skin care is done, and I am ready for bed.

Mom gently tucks me into bed, and kisses me goodnight. She says, "I love you Emma, and I am proud of you for taking such good care of your skin today!"

I close my eyes and lie quietly between the cool sheets. It feels good to have my ezcema under control. Someday I might even outgrow it!

Good Night, Emma!

Dear Loving Adult,

As you may know, eczema can be an emotional roller coaster for both you and your child. Feelings of helplessness, confusion, frustration, and hope are a normal experience as you tackle the persistent itch. A child's emotional experience is different from ours, and they may not have the maturity or language skills to express what they feel.

"I Have Eczema" is intended to give children a picture of eczema, by showing a young girl going through the same experience. Children who understand their eczema, triggers, and treatments are more likely to feel in control. Empowering children in this way makes the emotional roller coaster smoother for the whole family.

This book was written for my daughter who has a moderate case of eczema. It has been amazing to watch her gain emotional control over her treatments and triggers.

In the book, and in our home, we call triggers 'Itchy Monsters'. This is a great way to add a little lightheartedness to an otherwise frustrating condition.

As you discover what treatments work for your child, my hope is that your whole family will gain strength, control, and coping tools from this book as you navigate life with eczema.

Jen Greatsinger

Jen Greatsinger, RN

Author Biographies
Middle River Studios, LLC

Jen Greatsinger

Jen Greatsinger received her Bachelor of Science in nursing from the College of St. Scholastica, Duluth, MN. She has worked as a county health nurse in the Nurse Family Partnership program, and also in pediatric home care.

Jen currently embraces country living in northern Wisconsin where she lives on the Middle River with her husband, three children, and thirteen chickens. Her oldest daughter has eczema.

Lisa Crosby (Jen's mother)

Lisa Crosby received her Bachelor of Fine Arts from Rockford College, Rockford, IL, and her Bachelor of Science in social work from the University of Wisconsin, Superior, WI. She currently works as a greeting card designer and font artist, and has worked in a variety of settings as a medical social worker.

Lisa lives on the shores of Superior Bay in northern Wisconsin with her husband and thier chocolate Labradoodle, Hershey.

SOOTHING

WET DRESSINGS

ALLERGIES

BATH

DRY SKIN

ITCHY

LOTION

MOISTURIZ

SCRATCHING

SKIN CARE

ECZEMA

EMOTION

TREATMENTS

ATOPIC DERMATITIS

HEAL

FEELINGS

TRIGGERS

RASHY

CREAM

DERMATOLOGIST

RED

OINTMENT

Made in the USA
Coppell, TX
29 September 2022

83779167R00019